Simple and Tasty
Soups, Stews
and Chowders

Devlin Throckmorton

Edition v1.04 (2021.06.10)

Table of Contents

Cold Soups

Watermelon Soup

1 ½ pounds seedless watermelon, diced and chilled

2 tablespoons lime juice, freshly squeezed

1 tablespoons fresh mint, chopped

2 teaspoons extra-virgin olive oil

Tabasco, to taste

Salt, to taste

Mint leaves for garnish

Put the diced watermelon, lime juice, mint leaves and olive oil in a blender. Mix until it is very smooth. Pour the mixture into a fine strainer. Strain the watermelon puree, pressing lightly on the solids to get out the watermelon juice but not getting any of the pulp.

Transfer the watermelon soup to a pitcher and season with Tabasco and salt. Refrigerate until the soup is well-chilled (at least 20 minutes). Serve the soup in bowls, garnished with mint leaves.

Chilled Cucumber Soup

4 large cucumbers (3 coarsely chopped, 1 peeled and diced)

½ cup ice cubes

¼ cup cold water

¼ cup extra-virgin olive oil

1 teaspoon fresh lemon juice

1 jalapeño, seeded and finely chopped

2 tablespoons mint leaves, shredded

Salt to taste

½ cup celery leaves, blanched and finely chopped

¼ cup plain Greek yogurt

Extra-virgin olive oil, for drizzling

In a blender, combine the chopped cucumbers, ice, water, olive oil, lemon juice, and half each of the jalapeño and mint and puree. Season with salt and refrigerate until cold.

Pour the cucumber soup into bowls and garnish with the diced cucumber, celery leaves, yogurt, and the remaining jalapeño and mint. Drizzle the soup with olive oil and serve.

Peach & Goat Cheese Soup

4 large peaches, peeled and sliced

¼ cup cucumber, peeled and finely diced

¼ cup yellow bell pepper, finely diced

¼ cup dried apricots, diced

2 tablespoons honey

3 tablespoons crumbled fresh goat cheese, plus more for garnish

¼ cup white balsamic vinegar, plus more for seasoning

¼ cup extra-virgin olive oil

2 tablespoons extra-virgin olive oil, plus more for drizzling

Kosher salt

1 clove garlic

2 cups diced baguette, crouton size

Basil leaves, for garnish

Freshly ground black pepper

In a large mixing bowl, toss the peaches, diced cucumber, yellow pepper, and apricots. Next, add the honey, 3 tablespoons of goat cheese, ¼ cup of balsamic vinegar, and 2 tablespoons of the olive oil. Stir in 1 ½ teaspoons of salt. Add the garlic. Cover and refrigerate overnight.

Discard the garlic. Place the contents of the bowl in a blender and puree. Add ¼ cup of water and puree until very smooth and creamy; add more water if the soup seems too thick. Season with salt and vinegar. Refrigerate the soup until cold, about 1 hour.

In a medium skillet, heat the remaining ¼ cup of olive oil. Add the diced bread and cook over moderate heat, stirring, until golden and crisp, about 2 minutes. Using a slotted spoon, transfer the croutons to paper towels and season with salt.

Pour the peach soup into individual bowls and garnish with sliced cucumber, sliced bell pepper, goat cheese, croutons, and basil. Drizzle lightly with olive oil, season with black pepper and serve.

Cantaloupe Soup

1 large cantaloupe, peeled, seeded and cubed

2 cups orange juice

1 tablespoon lime juice

½ teaspoon ground cinnamon

Fresh mint, chopped

In blender or food processor blend together melon and juice until smooth.

Place in large bowl and stir in lime juice and cinnamon.

Cover and chill for at least 1 hour.

Sprinkle with mint to garnish and serve

Gazpacho

4 cups tomato juice

1 onion, minced

1 green bell pepper, minced

1 cucumber, chopped

2 cups chopped tomatoes

2 green onions, chopped

1 clove garlic, minced

3 tablespoons fresh lemon juice

2 tablespoons red wine vinegar

1 teaspoon dried tarragon

1 teaspoon dried basil

¼ cup chopped fresh parsley

1 teaspoon white sugar

Salt and pepper to taste

In a blender or food processor, combine tomato juice, onion, bell pepper, cucumber, tomatoes, green onions, garlic, lemon juice, red wine vinegar, tarragon, basil, parsley, sugar, salt, and pepper. Blend until well-combined but still slightly chunky. Chill at least 2 hours before serving.

Sweet Potato Soup

3 large sweet potatoes

3 (14 ounce) cans low-sodium chicken broth

¼ cup brown sugar, or more to taste

½ teaspoon salt

¼ teaspoon ground nutmeg

Black pepper to taste

Cayenne pepper to taste

1/3 cup heavy cream

Preheat oven to 350 degrees.

Bake sweet potatoes in preheated oven until soft, about 1 ½ hours. Remove and let cool slightly.

Peel the sweet potatoes, and puree together with chicken broth in small batches, using enough chicken broth so that it purees smoothly. Bring puree to a simmer in a large saucepan over medium-high heat, then reduce heat to medium-low. Stir in the sugar, salt, nutmeg, black pepper, and cayenne pepper; cover, and let simmer for 10 minutes. Remove from heat, and stir in cream.

Avocado Cilantro Soup

3 large ripe avocadoes, peeled and pitted

3 cups chicken broth

1 tablespoon fresh lime juice

2/3 cup plain yogurt

1/3 cup sour cream

1 large tomato, peeled and seeded

¼ cup chopped fresh cilantro

Salt, to taste

Tabasco sauce, for serving

In a blender or a food processor, combine 2 of the avocados, the stock or broth, lime juice, yogurt, and sour cream. Blend until smooth.

Add the tomato and cilantro. Pulse until the tomato is coarsely chopped, not puree.

Pour into a bowl and season with salt. Coarsely chop the remaining avocado half and stir into the soup. Refrigerate for at least 2 hours. Ladle into bowls and serve with a dash of hot sauce.

Cream Soups

Cream of Asparagus and Mushroom Soup

3 slices bacon

1 tablespoon bacon drippings

¼ cup butter

3 stalks celery, chopped

1 onion, diced

3 tablespoons all-purpose flour

6 cups chicken broth

1 potato, peeled and diced

1 pound fresh asparagus, tips set aside and stalks chopped

Salt and ground black pepper to taste

1 (8 ounce) package sliced fresh mushrooms

¾ cup half-and-half cream

Place the bacon in a large, deep skillet, and cook over medium-high heat, turning occasionally, until evenly browned, about 10 minutes. Drain the bacon slices on a paper towel-lined plate. Crumble bacon when cool; set aside. Reserve 1 tablespoon of bacon drippings.

Melt butter with drippings in a saucepan over medium heat.

Cook and stir celery and onion in the saucepan until onion is translucent, about 4 minutes.

Whisk flour into the mixture and cook for 1 minute.

Whisk in chicken broth and bring to a boil.

Add potato and chopped asparagus stalks, reserving the asparagus tips for later. Season with salt and ground black pepper.

Reduce heat and simmer for 20 minutes.

Puree in batches until smooth and pour into a clean pot. Alternately, you can use a stick blender and puree the soup right in the cooking pot.

Cook and stir mushrooms and asparagus tips in the same skillet used for bacon until mushrooms give up their liquid, 5 to 8 minutes. Season with salt and ground black pepper, if needed.

Stir mushrooms, asparagus tips, and half-and-half cream to pureed soup. Cook until thoroughly heated.

Garnish soup with crumbled bacon.

Tomato Basil Soup

4 cups canned whole tomatoes, crushed

4 cups tomato juice (part chicken stock)

12 basil leaves, washed fresh

1 cup heavy cream

¼ pound sweet unsalted butter

Salt

¼ teaspoon cracked black pepper

Lemon juice (optional)

Combine tomatoes, juice and or stock in saucepan. Simmer 30 minutes.

Puree, along with the basil leaves, in small batches, in blender. Return to saucepan and add cream and butter, while stirring, over low heat. Garnish with basil leaves and serve with your favorite bread.

Cream of Mushroom Soup

½ pound fresh mushrooms, cleaned and chopped

6 tablespoons butter

2/3 cup flour

2 quarts chicken broth

1 cup half-and-half cream or 1 cup milk

Lightly sauté mushrooms in butter. Add flour and stir constantly for about 5 minutes.

Slowly add stock, stirring until all is incorporated. Simmer about 10 minutes.

Add cream, stir and serve.

Cream of Chicken and Wild Rice Soup

3 ½ cups chicken broth

1 cup sliced carrot

½ cup sliced celery

1/3 cup wild rice

1/3 cup sliced onion

½ teaspoon dried thyme

2 tablespoons butter

3 tablespoons flour

1 cup half-and-half cream

1 ½ cups cut-up cooked chicken

Mix broth, carrots, celery, uncooked rice, onions, thyme, and ¼ teaspoon pepper.

Bring to a boil; reduce heat, cover and simmer 1 hour, until the rice is tender.

Melt butter, stir in the flour, then the half-half.

Cook and stir 1 minute. Slowly add half-half mixture to the rice mixture, stirring constantly. Stir in the chicken and heat through.

Broccoli Cheese Soup

½ cup butter

1 onion, chopped

1 (16 ounce) package frozen chopped broccoli

4 (14.5 ounce) cans chicken broth

1 (1 pound) loaf processed cheese food, cubed

2 cups milk

1 tablespoon garlic powder

2/3 cup cornstarch

1 cup water

In a stockpot, melt butter over medium heat. Cook onion in butter until softened. Stir in broccoli, and cover with chicken broth. Simmer until broccoli is tender, 10 to 15 minutes.

Reduce heat, and stir in cheese cubes until melted. Mix in milk and garlic powder.

In a small bowl, stir cornstarch into water until dissolved. Stir into soup; cook, stirring frequently, until thick.

Hearty Soups

Italian Wedding Soup

1 pound extra-lean ground beef

2 eggs, beaten

¼ cup dried bread crumbs

2 tablespoons grated Parmesan cheese

1 teaspoon dried basil

3 tablespoons minced onion

2 ½ quarts chicken broth

2 cups spinach — packed, rinsed and thinly sliced

1 cup seashell pasta

¾ cup diced carrots

In a medium bowl, combine the beef, egg, bread crumbs, cheese, basil and onion. Shape mixture into ¾-inch balls and set aside.

In a large stockpot heat chicken broth to boiling; stir in the spinach, pasta, carrot and meatballs. Return to boil; reduce heat to medium. Cook, stirring frequently, at a slow boil for 10 minutes or until pasta is al dente, and meatballs are no longer pink inside. Serve hot with Parmesan cheese sprinkled on top.

Ham and Potato Soup

3 ½ cups peeled and diced potatoes

1/3 cup diced celery

1/3 cup finely chopped onion

¾ cup diced cooked ham

3 ¼ cups water

2 tablespoons chicken bouillon granules

½ teaspoon salt, or to taste

1 teaspoon ground white or black pepper, or to taste

5 tablespoons butter

5 tablespoons all-purpose flour

2 cups milk

Combine the potatoes, celery, onion, ham and water in a stockpot. Bring to a boil, then cook over medium heat until potatoes are tender, about 10 to 15 minutes. Stir in the chicken bouillon, salt and pepper.

In a separate saucepan, melt butter over medium-low heat. Whisk in flour with a fork, and cook, stirring constantly until thick, about 1 minute. Slowly stir in milk as not to allow lumps to form until all of the milk has been added. Continue stirring over medium-low heat until thick, 4 to 5 minutes.

Stir the milk mixture into the stockpot, and cook soup until heated through. Serve immediately.

Minestrone

3 tablespoons olive oil

3 cloves garlic, chopped

2 onions, chopped

2 cups chopped celery

5 carrots, sliced

2 cups chicken broth

2 cups water

4 cups tomato sauce

½ cup red wine (optional)

1 cup canned kidney beans, drained

1 (15 ounce) can green beans

2 cups baby spinach, rinsed

3 zucchinis, quartered and sliced

1 tablespoon chopped fresh oregano

2 tablespoons chopped fresh basil

Salt and pepper to taste

½ cup seashell pasta

2 tablespoons grated Parmesan cheese for topping

1 tablespoon olive oil

In a large stock pot, over medium-low heat, heat olive oil and sauté garlic for 2 to 3 minutes. Add onion and sauté for 4 to 5 minutes. Add celery and carrots, sauté for 1 to 2 minutes.

Add chicken broth, water and tomato sauce, bring to boil, stirring frequently. If desired add red wine at this point. Reduce heat to low and add kidney beans, green beans, spinach leaves, zucchini, oregano, basil, salt and pepper. Simmer for 30 to 40 minutes, the longer the better.

Fill a medium saucepan with water and bring to a boil. Add macaroni and cook until tender. Drain water and set aside.

Once pasta is cooked and soup is heated through place 2 tablespoons cooked pasta into individual serving bowls. Ladle soup on top of pasta and sprinkle Parmesan cheese on top. Spray with olive oil and serve.

Italian Sausage Soup

1 pound sweet Italian sausage, casings removed

1 cup chopped onion

2 cloves garlic, minced

5 cups beef broth

½ cup water

½ cup red wine

4 large tomatoes — peeled, seeded and chopped

1 cup thinly sliced carrots

½ tablespoon packed fresh basil leaves

½ teaspoon dried oregano

1 (8 ounce) can tomato sauce

1 ½ cups sliced zucchini

8 ounces fresh tortellini pasta

3 tablespoons chopped fresh parsley

In a 5 quart Dutch oven, brown sausage. Remove sausage and drain, reserving 1 tablespoon of the drippings. Sauté onions and garlic in drippings. Stir in beef broth, water, wine, tomatoes, carrots, basil, oregano, tomato sauce, and sausage. Bring to a boil. Reduce heat; simmer uncovered for 30 minutes.

Skim fat from the soup. Stir in zucchini and parsley. Simmer covered for 30 minutes. Add tortellini during the last 10 minutes. Sprinkle with Parmesan cheese on top of each serving.

Chicken Noodle Soup

2 ½ cups wide egg noodles

1 teaspoon vegetable oil

12 cups chicken broth

1 ½ tablespoons salt

 1 teaspoon poultry seasoning

1 cup chopped celery

1 cup chopped onion

1/3 cup cornstarch

¼ cup water

3 cups diced, cooked chicken meat

Bring a large pot of lightly salted water to a boil. Add egg noodles and oil, and boil for 8 minutes, or until tender. Drain, and rinse under cool running water.

In a large saucepan or Dutch oven, combine broth, salt, and poultry seasoning. Bring to a boil. Stir in celery and onion. Reduce heat, cover, and simmer 15 minutes.

In a small bowl, mix cornstarch and water together until cornstarch is completely dissolved. Gradually add to soup, stirring constantly. Stir in noodles and chicken, and heat through.

Potato Soup

1 pound bacon, chopped

2 stalks celery, diced

1 onion, chopped

3 cloves garlic, minced

8 potatoes, peeled and cubed

4 cups chicken stock, or enough to cover potatoes

3 tablespoons butter

¼ cup all-purpose flour

1 cup heavy cream

1 teaspoon dried tarragon

3 teaspoons chopped fresh cilantro

Salt and pepper to taste

In a Dutch oven, cook the bacon over medium heat until done. Remove bacon from pan, and set aside. Drain off all but ¼ cup of the bacon grease.

In the bacon grease remaining in the pan, sauté the celery and onion until onion begins to turn clear.

Add the garlic, and continue cooking for 1 to 2 minutes. Add the cubed potatoes, and toss to coat. Sauté for 3 to 4 minutes. Return the bacon to the pan, and add enough chicken stock to just cover the potatoes. Cover, and simmer until potatoes are tender.

In a separate pan, melt the butter over medium heat. Whisk in the flour. Cook stirring constantly, for 1 to 2 minutes. Whisk in the heavy cream, tarragon and cilantro. Bring the cream mixture to a boil, and cook, stirring constantly, until thickened. Stir the cream mixture into the potato mixture. Puree about ½ the soup, and return to the pan. Adjust seasonings to taste.

Chicken Tortilla Soup

1 onion, chopped

3 cloves garlic, minced

1 tablespoon olive oil

2 teaspoons chili powder

1 teaspoon dried oregano

1 (28 ounce) can crushed tomatoes

1 (10.5 ounce) can condensed chicken broth

1 ¼ cups water

1 cup whole corn kernels, cooked

1 cup white hominy

1 (4 ounce) can chopped green chili peppers

1 (15 ounce) can black beans, rinsed and drained

¼ cup chopped fresh cilantro

2 boneless chicken breast halves, cooked and cut into bite-sized pieces

Crushed tortilla chips

Sliced avocado

Shredded Monterey Jack cheese

Chopped green onions

In a medium stock pot, heat oil over medium heat. Sauté onion and garlic in oil until soft. Stir in chili powder, oregano, tomatoes, broth, and water. Bring to a boil, and simmer for 5 to 10 minutes.

Stir in corn, hominy, chiles, beans, cilantro, and chicken. Simmer for 10 minutes. Ladle soup into individual serving bowls, and top with crushed tortilla chips, avocado slices, cheese, and chopped green onion.

Chicken and Dumplings

2 (10.75 ounce) cans condensed cream of chicken soup

3 cups water

1 cup chopped celery

2 onions, quartered

1 teaspoon salt

½ teaspoon poultry seasoning

½ teaspoon ground black pepper

4 skinless, boneless chicken breast halves

5 carrots, sliced

1 (10 ounce) package frozen green peas

4 potatoes, quartered

3 cups baking mix

1 1/3 cups milk

In large, heavy pot, combine soup, water, chicken, celery, onion, salt, poultry seasoning, and pepper. Cover and cook over low heat about 1 ½ hours.

Add potatoes and carrots; cover and cook another 30 minutes.

Remove chicken from pot, shred it, and return to pot. Add peas and cook only 5 minutes longer.

Add dumplings.

To make dumplings: Mix baking mix and milk until a soft dough forms. Drop by tablespoonfuls onto BOILING stew. Simmer covered for 10 minutes, then uncover and simmer an additional 10 minutes.

Split Pea and Ham Soup

8 cups water

1 large ham bone

2 cups dried split green peas

2 large carrots, peeled and diced small

2 medium onions, chopped small

2 large celery ribs, include leaves, chop small

1 large bay leaf

2 beef bouillon cubes

1 teaspoon salt

¼ teaspoon black peppercorns, crushed

1 pinch dried thyme

Rinse peas well in cold water and add to a large cooking pot. Measure 8 cups of water and add to cooking pot. Bring to boil, remove from heat, cover and let sit for 1 hour.

Return to stove and bring back to boil. Add ham bone, carrots, onions, celery, bay leaf, beef bouillon, salt, peppercorns and dried thyme.

Reduce heat to simmer, cover and cook for about 1 to 1 ½ hours, stirring occasionally.

Remove ham bone and cut off any remaining ham, cut into bite size pieces and return to soup.

Discard ham bone. If there are big pieces of ham in the soup, remove, cut into bite size pieces and return to soup.

Remove bay leaf and discard. Adjust seasonings to taste.

If you desire a smooth soup, then puree in batches in a food processor or blender.

Or eat the soup without pureeing.

If soup is too thick, add more water to your desired consistency. Beef broth or chicken broth may be added, just reduce the water by the amounts used.

Smoked ham hocks are excellent to use instead of a ham bone.

French Onion Soup

4 cups thinly sliced onions

½ tablespoon sugar

¼ teaspoon pepper

¼ cup vegetable oil

4 cups beef broth

4 slices French bread, toasted

½ cup shredded Swiss cheese

In soup pot, cook onions, sugar, and pepper in oil until caramelized (about 15-20 minutes). Stir often.

Add broth; bring to a boil. Reduce heat; cover and simmer for 20 minutes.

Ladle into ovenproof bowls. Top each with bread and cheese. Broil until cheese is bubbly.

Tuscan White Bean & Spinach Soup

2 teaspoons olive oil

1 garlic clove, finely minced

1 shallot, finely diced

3 to 4 cups chicken broth

1 (14 ½ ounce) can diced tomatoes

1 (14 ½ ounce) can white beans

½ cup pasta shells

1 teaspoon rosemary

3 cups spinach, cleaned and trimmed

1/8 teaspoon black pepper

1 dash crushed red pepper flakes

In a large sauce pan, sauté the shallots & garlic in the olive oil.

Add broth, tomatoes, beans and rosemary to pot. Season with black and red pepper. Bring to boil.

Add pasta and cook 12 minutes. If the soup seems too thick for your liking add a bit more broth.

Add spinach and cook until wilted.

Meatball Soup

For the meatballs:

½ pound lean ground beef

½ pound chorizo

1 egg, beaten

2 garlic cloves, minced

½ carrot, minced

½ cup cooked rice

½ cup cilantro leaf, chopped

½ teaspoon salt

¼ teaspoon pepper

1 teaspoon ground cumin

For the soup:

6 cups chicken broth

½ cup onion, chopped

3 stalks celery, cut in chunks

1 (16 ounce) can diced tomatoes

½ teaspoon ground cumin

1 teaspoon oregano

½ cup cilantro

1 large zucchini, sliced

Salt and pepper to taste

Make the meatballs first:

Combine everything and mix thoroughly. Form meatballs and roll between your palms. Recipe makes about 20 meatballs. Set aside.

Make the soup:

Combine chicken broth, onion, celery, tomatoes, cumin, oregano and cilantro leaves in a large pot.

Bring to broil, and reduce heat and simmer for 10 minutes. Drop meatballs in the soup. Return to simmer and cook another 10 minutes.

Add zucchini and cook 10 minutes. Season with salt and pepper, to taste.

Pasta e Fagioli

1 tablespoon olive oil

1 onion, chopped

2 cloves garlic, finely chopped

1 carrot, peeled & chopped

1 stalk celery, chopped

1 pound sweet Italian sausage links

2 teaspoons dry oregano

1 tablespoon dry basil

1 teaspoon red pepper flakes, to taste

1 ½ cups canned chopped tomatoes with juice

3 to 4 cups chicken broth

1 can cannellini beans

1 cup ditalini

2 tablespoons chopped flat leaf parsley

Parmesan cheese

Heat olive oil in a large heavy pot over medium high heat. Cook onion in oil 2 minutes. Stir in garlic, celery and carrots and cook for 3 minutes. Add and brown crumbled sausage. Add basil, oregano and red pepper. Toss to coat.

Stir in tomatoes and stock. Bring to a boil. Reduce heat and simmer 30 minutes. If necessary, add an additional cup of stock or water and stir in beans and tiny pasta.

Simmer for 6- 8 minutes or until pasta is tender. Stir in parsley and serve hot with grated Parmesan cheese.

Lemon Chicken Rice Soup

6 cups chicken broth

1 chicken bouillon cube

1/3 cup rice, uncooked

1/3 cup carrot, diced

1/3 cup celery, chopped

¼ cup onion, finely chopped

1 cup chicken, cubed and cooked

2 tablespoons butter

2 tablespoons flour

3 eggs

3 tablespoons lemon juice

Salt and pepper

Lemon slice (optional)

Sliced green onions or parsley (optional)

In a large saucepan, combine chicken broth, bouillon cube, rice, carrots, celery and onion. Bring to a boil.

Reduce heat, cover and simmer 20 minutes or until rice and vegetables are tender. Stir in chicken. Remove from heat.

Then, in a small saucepan, melt butter and stir in flour until smooth. Gradually add 2 cups of broth mixture, cook until slightly thickened, stirring constantly.

In a small bowl, beat the eggs until frothy. Gradually beat lemon juice and 2 cups thickened broth into the large pot of soup.

Very slowly add egg mixture into the soup, stirring constantly. Do not do this if your soup is boiling or very hot or your eggs will split. You may want to take the soup off the burner for a few minutes before you add the eggs.

Heat gently until soup thickens enough to coat a spoon—do not boil! Add salt and pepper to taste, garnish with lemon.

15 Bean Soup

1 (1 pound) bag regular 15 bean soup mix

1 large onion, chopped

4 garlic cloves, minced

1 (15 -30 ounce) can whole tomatoes, crushed

3 stalks celery leaves, included chopped

2 -3 ham hocks or 1 ham bone, with meat still on it

1 tablespoon dried parsley

1 teaspoon dried rosemary

1 teaspoon black pepper

Salt

2 tablespoons olive oil

2   chicken bouillon cubes

Wash the beans; put in large pot and cover with water. Bring to boil; stir and remove from heat. Cover and let sit 1 hour. After that hour, drain beans and set aside.

Add oil to pot. Sauté your ham hocks, onion, and celery until tender.

Next add garlic and sauté 2 minutes more.

Add your beans and cover with water (about 2 inches over top of beans).

Add tomatoes with the juice, parsley, rosemary, black pepper, bouillon cubes, and about 1 teaspoon of salt to start with.

Mix well. Bring to boil; stir, reduce heat cover and simmer for 2 to 2 ½ hours or until all the sizes of the beans are tender.

Keep watching it and stirring it every once in a while. You may need to add more water; you want it to keep a consistency a little thicker than a soup.

Taste it after it cooks. Add salt as needed

Garlic Lentil Soup

1 cup red lentil, rinsed and drained

2 onions, finely chopped

2 garlic cloves

1 carrot, thinly sliced

2 tablespoons olive oil

2 bay leaves

1 pinch dried marjoram or 1 pinch oregano

6 ¼ cups vegetable stock

2 tablespoons red wine vinegar

 Salt and pepper

Put the lentils, onions, garlic, carrot, oil, bay leaves, marjoram or oregano and stock into a large saucepan.

Bring to the boil and then simmer gently for 1 ½ hours, stirring occasionally.

Remove bay leaves and add the red wine vinegar as well as the salt and pepper to taste.

You can thin the soup out if you like with a little stock or water before serving.

Meatball and Spinach Soup

4 cups chicken broth (or 2 cans)

1 pound ground beef

¼ cup parmesan cheese

1/8 teaspoon ground black pepper

1 (10 ounce) package frozen spinach

Heat chicken broth to boiling.

Meanwhile, combine beef, cheese and pepper.

Knead lightly to mix but don't overdo it.

Roll into 1 inch meatballs.

Drop meatballs into boiling broth and reduce heat to simmering (medium low usually).

Cook for 10 minutes. Add spinach and cook for 10 more minutes.

Serve with French bread if you have it

Tomato & Barley Soup

1 cup onion (diced)

1 cup carrot (diced)

1 cup celery (diced)

2 teaspoons garlic (minced)

2 tablespoons olive oil

1/3 cup pearl barley

1 (14 ounce) can stewed tomatoes

2 cups chicken broth

2 cups water

1 bay leaf

1/8 teaspoon black pepper

Heat the olive oil in a large pot.

Add the onions, carrots, celery and garlic. Sauté for about 10 minutes or until the vegetables are starting to soften.

While they are cooking pour the barley into a dish with water to cover.

Add the tomatoes, broth, water, bay leaf, and pepper and bring to a boil, stirring occasionally.

Drain the barley and add to the pot.

Reduce heat and cook at a low boil for about 45 minutes (until the barley is tender).

Add more water or broth if it thickens too much.

Chowders & Stews

Beef Stew

2 pounds cubed beef stew meat

3 tablespoons vegetable oil

4 cubes beef bouillon, crumbled

4 cups water

1 teaspoon dried rosemary

1 teaspoon dried parsley

½ teaspoon ground black pepper

3 large potatoes, peeled and cubed

4 carrots, cut into 1 inch pieces

4 stalks celery, cut into 1 inch pieces

1 large onion, chopped

2 teaspoons cornstarch

2 teaspoons cold water

In a large pot or Dutch oven, cook beef in oil over medium heat until brown. Dissolve bouillon in water and pour into pot. Stir in rosemary, parsley and pepper. Bring to a boil, then reduce heat, cover and simmer 1 hour.

Stir potatoes, carrots, celery, and onion into the pot. Dissolve cornstarch in 2 teaspoons cold water and stir into stew. Cover and simmer 1 hour more.

Clam Chowder

3 (6.5 ounce) cans minced clams

1 cup minced onion

1 cup diced celery

2 cups cubed potatoes

1 cup diced carrots

¾ cup butter

¾ cup all-purpose flour

1 quart half-and-half cream

2 tablespoons red wine vinegar

1 ½ teaspoons salt

Ground black pepper to taste

Drain juice from clams into a large skillet over the onions, celery, potatoes and carrots. Add water to cover, and cook over medium heat until tender.

Meanwhile, in a large, heavy saucepan, melt the butter over medium heat. Whisk in flour until smooth. Whisk in cream and stir constantly until thick and smooth. Stir in vegetables and clam juice. Heat through, but do not boil.

Stir in clams just before serving. If they cook too much they get tough. When clams are heated through, stir in vinegar, and season with salt and pepper.

Corn and Potato Chowder

2 ½ cups cooked corn

2 cups diced potatoes

1 tablespoon butter

¼ cup onion, diced

½ teaspoon salt

1/8 teaspoon pepper

1 ½ cups boiling water

2 cups hot milk

1 tablespoon flour, mixed with

1 tablespoon water

In a large pot, combine all ingredients except milk and flour/water.

Cook until potatoes are fork tender.

Add milk and flour/water, stirring well.

Bring to a boil and allow to cook for 10 minutes.

Serve with chopped green onion and shredded cheese as a garnish.

Seafood Chowder

½ cup butter

1 stalk celery, minced

1 small onion, minced

¼ teaspoon cayenne pepper

¼ teaspoon dried thyme

¼ teaspoon dried marjoram

3 tablespoons flour or 3 tablespoons baking mix

3 ½ cups milk

2 cans condensed cream of potato soup (undiluted)

1 ½ pounds shrimp or 1 ½ pounds scallops

Chopped fresh parsley (to garnish)

Melt butter in 3-quart saucepan over low heat.

Sauté celery and onion until tender.

Add cayenne pepper, thyme, marjoram and flour or baking mix and stir until smooth.

Add milk and condensed soup and stir until piping hot.

Meanwhile clean and chop seafood as you like.

When soup is piping hot add seafood and stir on medium heat until seafood is cooked through.

Serve in bowls topped with some fresh parsley along with some crusty bread or oyster crackers and a nice salad.

Crock Pot
Slow Cooker Soups

Crock Pot Chicken Noodle Soup

4 cups cooked chicken, chopped (from a store bought chicken?)

1 cup onion, diced

1 cup celery, diced

1 cup carrot, diced

½ cup frozen peas

4 (14 ounce) cans low sodium chicken broth

2 (10 ¾ ounce) cans condensed cream of mushroom soup (with roasted garlic)

2 teaspoons fines herbes (chervil, chives, parsley, and tarragon)

Salt

Pepper to taste

2 cups egg noodles, cooked

Remove skin from the chicken and chop the meat.

Put the chicken into a slow cooker with the onions, celery, carrots and peas.

Stir in broth, mushroom soup, and fines herbs. Season with salt and pepper.

Cover and cook on high for 3 to 4 hours or low for 8 to 9 hours.

When soup is finished, stir in egg noodles.

Season to taste and serve

Crock Pot Taco Soup

1 (16 ounce) can pinto beans

1 (16 ounce) can white beans or 1 (16 ounce) can kidney beans

1 (11 ounce) can niblet corn

1 (11 ounce) can Rotel tomatoes & chilies

1 (28 ounce) can diced tomatoes

1 (4 ounce) can diced green chilies

1 (1 ¼ ounce) envelope taco seasoning mix

1 (1 ounce) envelope ranch dressing and seasoning mix

1 pound shredded chicken, ground beef or 1 pound any meat

Cook meat and drain.

Shred if needed.

Add all ingredients to crock pot.

DO NOT DRAIN CANS.

Stir.

Cook on high for 2 hours or low for 4 hours.

Keep on low until serving to keep hot.

Garnish with sour cream, shredded cheese, chopped green onions, or tortilla chips

Slow Cooker Beef and Barley Soup

2 pounds beef round steak or 2 pounds beef chuck, diced

2 cups chopped carrots

1 stalk celery, diced

½ green pepper, diced

1 large onion, chopped

1 (16 ounce) can tomatoes, cut up

½ cup frozen corn

½ cup frozen green beans

2/3 cup barley

1 tablespoon dried parsley flakes

1 tablespoon beef bouillon granules or 2 beef bouillon cubes

2 teaspoons salt

¾ teaspoon dried basil

5 cups water

In skillet brown beef.

Place carrot, celery, green pepper, onion, corn and green beans in crock pot.

Put meat on top.

Combine tomatoes, barley, parsley, bouillon, salt and basil. Pour over meat. Add water.

DO NOT STIR. Cover and cook on LOW for 10-12 hours.

Crock Pot Baked Potato Soup

6 large baking potatoes, peeled, cut in ½ inch cubes

1 large onion, chopped

1 quart chicken broth

3 garlic cloves, minced (or pressed)

¼ cup butter

2 ½ teaspoons salt

1 teaspoon pepper

1 cup cream or 1 cup half-and-half cream

1 cup shredded sharp cheddar cheese

3 tablespoons chopped fresh chives

1 cup sour cream (optional)

8 slices bacon, fried and crumbled

Cheese, for sprinkling

Combine first seven ingredients in a large crock pot; cover and cook on HIGH for 4 hours or LOW for 8 hours (potato should be tender).

Mash mixture until potatoes are coarsely chopped and soupy is slightly thickened.

Stir in cream, cheese and chives.

Top with sour cream (if used), sprinkle with bacon and more cheese.

List of Soup:

15 Bean Soup 23

Avocado Cilantro Soup 6

Beef Stew 27

Broccoli Cheese Soup 10

Cantaloupe Soup 4

Chicken and Dumplings 17

Chicken Noodle Soup 14

Chicken Tortilla Soup 16

Chilled Cucumber Soup 3

Clam Chowder 27

Corn and Potato Chowder 28

Cream of Asparagus and Mushroom Soup 8

Cream of chicken and wild Rice Soup 10

Cream of Mushroom Soup 9

Crock Pot Baked Potato Soup 32

Crock Pot Chicken Noodle Soup 30

Crock Pot Taco Soup 30

French Onion Soup 19

Garlic Lentil Soup 24

Gazpacho 5

Ham and Potato Soup 12

Italian Sausage Soup 14

Italian Wedding Soup 12

Lemon Chicken Rice Soup 22

Meatball and Spinach Soup 24

Meatball Soup 20

Minestrone 13

Pasta E Fagioli 21

Peach Soup & Goat Cheese Soup 4

Potato Soup 15

Seafood Chowder 28

Slow Cooker Beef and Barley Soup 31

Split Pea and Ham Soup 18

Sweet Potato Soup 5

Tomato & Barley Soup 25

Tomato Basil Soup 9

Tuscan White Bean & Spinach Soup 19

Watermelon Soup 3